THIS SCRIPTURE JOURNAL
BELONGS TO

_____

_____

_____

LOVE YOUR JOURNAL?

Tag me in your social media posts and stories!
@myscripturejournal

I always appreciate reviews on my Amazon listings
to help spread the word about these journals.

More info at
myscripturejournal.com

All scripture is given by inspiration of God, and is profitable for doctrine, for reproof, for correction, for instruction in righteousness: That the man of God may be perfect, thoroughly furnished unto all good works.

2 Timothy 3:16-17

HOW TO USE THIS JOURNAL

1. Choose a page in this journal and write the date at the top.
2. Open whatever translation of the Bible you prefer.
3. Find the verse noted at the top of the journal page.
4. Write out the Bible verse.
5. Use the space on the facing page to write notes or reflections on the verse and write out your prayers for the day.

WHY WRITE OUT BIBLE VERSES

Writing is a deeper sensory experience than reading, typing or listening. Research shows that hand writing increases memory and retention.

Writing scripture is also a tradition of the faith. Before the advent of the printing press, scribes were tasked with writing copies of the scriptures by hand.

I pray that as you form each letter, you will be blessed deeply by the intention and attention that is required of the process.

IN CHRIST'S LOVE, EMILY FONTES

REFLECTION

PRAYER

REFLECTION

PRAYER

REFLECTION

PRAYER

REFLECTION

PRAYER

REFLECTION

PRAYER

REFLECTION

PRAYER

REFLECTION

PRAYER

REFLECTION

PRAYER

REFLECTION

PRAYER

REFLECTION

PRAYER

REFLECTION

PRAYER

REFLECTION

PRAYER

REFLECTION

PRAYER

SCRIPTURE   1 John 3:16-18

REFLECTION

PRAYER

REFLECTION

PRAYER

REFLECTION

PRAYER

REFLECTION

PRAYER

REFLECTION

PRAYER

REFLECTION

PRAYER

REFLECTION

PRAYER

REFLECTION

PRAYER

REFLECTION

PRAYER

SCRIPTURE   Hebrews 13:1-3

REFLECTION

PRAYER

REFLECTION

PRAYER

REFLECTION

PRAYER

REFLECTION

PRAYER

SCRIPTURE   Malachi 3:10-12

REFLECTION

PRAYER

REFLECTION

PRAYER

REFLECTION

PRAYER

REFLECTION

PRAYER

REFLECTION

PRAYER

REFLECTION

PRAYER

REFLECTION

PRAYER

REFLECTION

PRAYER

REFLECTION

PRAYER

REFLECTION

PRAYER

REFLECTION

PRAYER

REFLECTION

PRAYER

REFLECTION

PRAYER

REFLECTION

PRAYER

REFLECTION

PRAYER

REFLECTION

PRAYER

REFLECTION

PRAYER

REFLECTION

PRAYER

REFLECTION

PRAYER

REFLECTION

PRAYER

REFLECTION

PRAYER

REFLECTION

PRAYER

REFLECTION

PRAYER

REFLECTION

PRAYER

REFLECTION

PRAYER

REFLECTION

PRAYER

REFLECTION

PRAYER

REFLECTION

PRAYER

REFLECTION

PRAYER

SCRIPTURE   Matthew 5:38-42

REFLECTION

PRAYER

REFLECTION

PRAYER

REFLECTION

PRAYER

REFLECTION

PRAYER

REFLECTION

PRAYER

REFLECTION

PRAYER

REFLECTION

PRAYER

REFLECTION

PRAYER

GENEROSITY SCRIPTURE JOURNAL
INDEX OF VERSES

READY FOR YOUR NEXT SCRIPTURE JOURNAL?

Find these journals and more at
myscripturejournal.com

ANXIETY SCRIPTURE JOURNAL
67 pre-selected bible verses to transform anxiety
and depression into peace and hope.

GENEROSITY SCRIPTURE JOURNAL
63 pre-selected bible verses to help you learn
how to live life more generously.

100 DAY SCRIPTURE WRITING JOURNAL
100 pre-selected bible verses for
encouragement, wisdom, peace and joy.

FRUIT OF THE SPIRIT SCRIPTURE JOURNAL
54 pre-selected bible verses reflecting on love,
joy, peace, patience, kindness, goodness,
faithfulness, gentleness and self control.

Made in the USA
Monee, IL
08 January 2024

51233623R00072